nickelodeon

TALENT SHOW

Popcorn
ELT
Readers

New Words

What do these new words mean? Ask your teacher or use your dictionary.

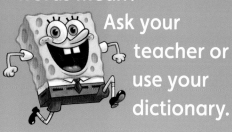

customer

There are a lot of **customers**.

buy

She is **buying** a book.

money

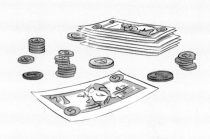

This is **money**.

clean up

He is **cleaning up**.

restaurant

He is eating in a **restaurant**.

star

She is a **star**.

talent show

It is a **talent show**.

throw

He is **throwing** a ball.

tomato

I like **tomatoes**.

work

He **works** in a kitchen.

'Hooray!' 'Boo!'

She likes the singer.

He doesn't like the singer.

CHAPTER ONE
'Where is everyone?'

SpongeBob is cleaning the tables in the Krusty Krab. Squidward is reading.

Mr Krabs is not happy. 'Where is everyone?' he says. 'No customers – no money! What can I do?'

'Let's have a talent show,' says Squidward.
'Pearl can dance.'

'Yes, my little girl is a star!' says Mr Krabs.

'Everyone loves talent shows!' says
Squidward.

'More customers – more money! Very good!' thinks Mr Krabs.

Squidward is very happy too.

'Pearl isn't the star of the show. I am!' he thinks. 'I've got talent. I can dance.'

'Can I be in the show?' asks SpongeBob.

'You?' Squidward laughs. 'No, you can't. You haven't got talent.'

'Yes I have. Look!' says SpongeBob.

'No, that's no good,' says Squidward.

'Look, Squidward!' says SpongeBob. 'I can do this! Can I be in the show now?'

'No,' says Squidward. 'But you can clean up after the show.'

CHAPTER TWO
Showtime!

It is the night of the talent show.

'Wow!' thinks SpongeBob. 'Everyone is here. Mum and Dad are talking to Mr Krabs! I love talent shows!'

'Come here, everyone,' says Squidward. 'Listen to me! This isn't your show, it's my show. I've got talent. It's my night!'

'And now it's showtime!' says Squidward to the customers. 'First we have Pearl. Look at her dance.'

'Wow!' says Mr Krabs. 'My little girl is a star.'

Pearl dances up and down. She is very big.
The customers go up and down with her.

'Look!' says Mr Krabs. 'She has got talent!'

AAAARRR!

'Now let's listen to Gary,' says Squidward.

The customers listen but they don't understand.

'Next we have Plankton,' says Squidward.
But Plankton is not very good ...

'Boo!' say the customers.

Plankton walks away quickly.

CHAPTER THREE
Talent and tomatoes

'The customers don't like the show,' says
Mr Krabs. 'Quick, Squidward! Do something!'

'OK, Mr Krabs,' says Squidward. 'I'm next
and I've got talent.'

Squidward dances but the customers are not happy. Someone throws a tomato at him.

'I don't want angry customers,' thinks Mr Krabs. 'Buy my tomatoes!' he shouts. The customers buy tomatoes and they throw them at Squidward.

'Good,' thinks Mr Krabs. 'I've got a lot of money now!'

Squidward stops. 'They don't like my dancing,' he thinks.

'Can I clean up now?' asks SpongeBob.

'Yes, you can,' Squidward says. 'There's no more show.'

CHAPTER FOUR
'He's a star!'

SpongeBob cleans up the tomatoes.
  'I like that,' says a customer.
  'That's good,' more customers say.
SpongeBob cleans quickly.
  'Hooray!' the customers shout.

HOORAY!

Squidward cannot see the customers but he listens to them.

'The customers want me again!' he thinks.

The customers see Squidward. They are not happy. The customers do not like Squidward, but they love SpongeBob!

Squidward is very angry but Mr Krabs is
very happy. He has lots of money!
'Thank you, Squidward,' he says.

SpongeBob's mum and dad are very happy too. 'My boy has got talent,' says SpongeBob's mum. 'He's a star!'

THE END

SEA SPONGES

A lot of people have sponges. But what is a sea sponge?

Living underwater

Sponges are not plants, they are animals! They live under the sea. They have no head, legs or arms. The sea water goes in and out of their bodies. Some sponges eat the small animals in the water.

How big?

Some sea sponges are very big – 2 metres tall or more!

Slow movers

A lot of sponges do not move but some young sponges can move very slowly (4mm in a day).

sea sponges

26

People and sponges

People take a lot of sponges from the sea. This is a problem because in some seas there are not many sponges now. Today many sponges in the home are not sea sponges. People make them.

Do you have a sponge? Is it a sea sponge?

Did you know ...?

Some sponges live for 200 years!

What do these words mean? Find out.

plants   bodies   move   people   take

After you read

1 True (✓) or False (✗)? Write in the box.

a) Mr Krabs likes money. ✓

b) Mr Krabs wants more customers. ☐

c) The customers like Plankton's show. ☐

d) Squidward dances in the show. ☐

e) Some customers buy Mr Krabs' tomatoes. ☐

f) SpongeBob sings in the talent show. ☐

2 Who says it? Write a name.

SpongeBob's mum   Mr Krabs   ~~Squidward~~
SpongeBob   Gary   a customer

a) 'I've got talent.' ....Squidward....

b) 'Can I be in the show?' ....

c) 'Meow!' ....

d) 'I've got a lot of money now!' ....

e) 'I like that.' ....

f) 'He's a star!' ....

Where's the popcorn?
Look in your book.
Can you find it?

Puzzle time!

1 Follow the lines and complete the sentences.

b) Squidward is reading a ....book............ .

a) Mr Krabs has lots of ....

c) SpongeBob is cleaning a ....

d) Gary is not a ....

e) A customer throws a ....

2 Make words from the letters in the tomatoes. The words are from pages 4 and 5.

a  b  c

a) t_ _ m _ _ o (good food!)

b) m _ _ _ y (rich men have a lot!)

c) t _ l _ n _ (good singers and dancers have it!)

3 Use the words and write the sentence.

~~Krusty Krab~~

a

the

~~talent~~

is

at

~~There~~

show

There ....

talent ....

.... Krusty Krab.

4 Ask and answer the questions with your friends.

	☺	☺	☹
Can you dance?	Yes!	Not sure ...	No!
Can you sing?	Yes!	Not sure ...	No!
Are you funny?	Yes!	Sometimes	No!
Can you walk on your hands?	Yes!	Not sure ...	No!

Everyone has talent! What can you do? Write a sentence.

I can ....

....

Imagine...

Work in pairs. Choose a character from the talent show. Who are you? What are you doing? Your friend guesses the answers.

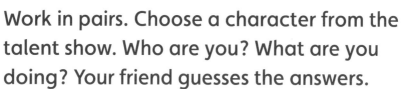

Who am I?

You are SpongeBob SquarePants!

What am I doing?

You are cleaning up!

Chant

1 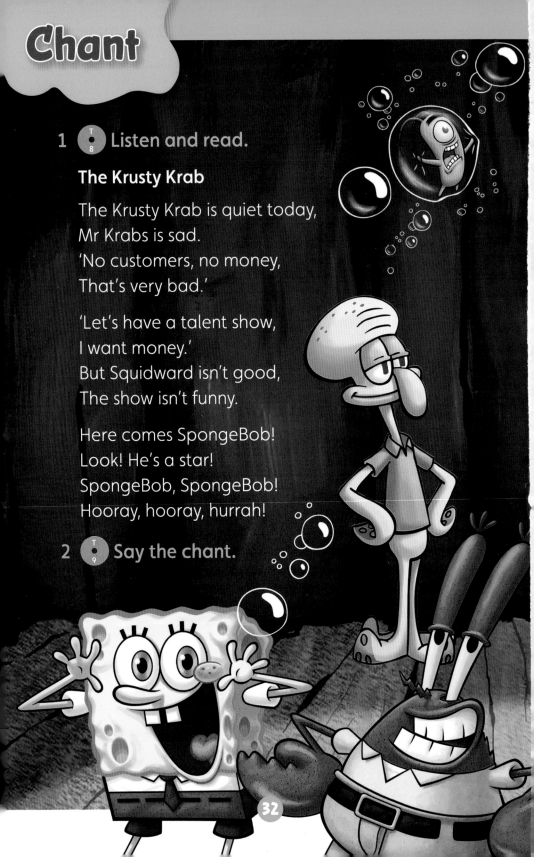 Listen and read.

The Krusty Krab

The Krusty Krab is quiet today,
Mr Krabs is sad.
'No customers, no money,
That's very bad.'

'Let's have a talent show,
I want money.'
But Squidward isn't good,
The show isn't funny.

Here comes SpongeBob!
Look! He's a star!
SpongeBob, SpongeBob!
Hooray, hooray, hurrah!

2 Say the chant.